The Amazing World of
INSECTS and SPIDERS

written by Lori C. Froeb
reviewed by Louis N. Sorkin, B.C.E.

Silver Dolphin
San Diego, California

Silver Dolphin Books
An imprint of the Baker & Taylor Publishing Group
10350 Barnes Canyon Road, San Diego, CA 92121
www.silverdolphinbooks.com

Copyright ©2013 Reader's Digest Children's Publishing, Inc.
All rights reserved.
"Silver Dolphin" is a registered trademark of Baker & Taylor. All rights reserved.
ISBN-13: 978-1-62686-013-1
ISBN-10: 1-62686-013-0
Manufactured, printed, and assembled in China.
1 2 3 4 5 17 16 15 14 13
FC/02/14

ILLUSTRATION AND PHOTOGRAPH CREDITS
(t=top, b=bottom, l=left, r=right, c=center)

Front Cover: Rob Mancini; **Pages 4, 5:** *Ray Grinaway 4,5c;* ©iStockphoto.com/Marcus Jones 5tr;
Pages 6, 7: *Ray Grinaway 6br; Ian Jackson/Wildlife Art 6,7c;* ©iStockphoto.com/Milos Luzanin 7tr;
Pages 8, 9: *Ian Jackson/Wildlife Art 8bl; Chris Shields/Wildlife Art 8,9c;* ©2008 Johan Swanepoel/Shutterstock.com 9tr;
Pages 10, 11: ©2008 Christopher Waters/Shutterstock.com bl; *Kevin Stead 10,11c;*
Pages 12, 13: *Rob Mancini bl;* ©2008 Cathy Keifer/Shutterstock.com 13tr; *Sandra Doyle/Wildlife Art 13br;*
Pages 14, 15: *Kevin Stead 14bl;* ©iStockphoto.com/arlindo71 15tr; *Ray Grinaway 15br;*
Pages 16, 17: ©iStockphoto.com/AravindTeki bl; *Kevin Stead 16, 17b; Steve Roberts/Wildlife Art 17tr;*
Pages 18, 19: ©iStockphoto com/CathyKeifer 19tr; **Pages 20, 21:** *Rob Mancini:20bl,* 20,21c;
Pages 22, 23: *Rob Mancini 22bl: 22br; Sandra Doyle/Wildlife Art 22,23c;* ©2008 Cathy Keifer/Shutterstock.com 23tr;
Pages 24, 25: *Sandra Doyle/Wildlife Art 24bl, 25tr;* ©2008 Snowleopard1/Shutterstock.com 25br;
Pages 26, 27: *Ray Grinaway 26bl, 27br;* ©iStockphoto.com/arlindo71 27tr; **Pages 28, 29:** ©2008 Ra'id Khalil/Shutterstock.com 28bl;
Rob Mancini 28,29c, 29r; **Pages 30, 31:** ©2008 Cathy Keifer/Shutterstock.com 30bl; *Ray Grinaway 31br; Dick Twinney 315tr;*
Pages 32, 33: *Chris Shields/Wildlife Art 32bl;* ©iStockphoto.com/Cathy Keifer 33tc; **Pages 34, 35:** ©2008 Leatha J. Robinson/
Shutterstock.com 34bl; *James McKinnon 35c; Anne Bowman 35tl;* **Page 37:** *Sandra Doyle/Wildlife Art*

Illustrations italicized above © 2000 Weldon Owen, Inc.

Diorama Imagery: ©Simon Baylis, ©INSAGO, ©JoeFotoSS, ©LilKar, ©Kittisak, ©phildaint, ©schankz, ©Sofiaworld, ©Bayanova Svetlana, ©Mary Terriberry, ©Birute Vijeikiene, ©Valentyn Volkov, ©Pan Xunbin, ©yuyangc/Shutterstock.com

Stickers: ©asharkyu, ©Le Do, ©Igor Gorelchenkov, ©Butterfly Hunter, ©irin-k, ©Eric Isselee, ©Kletr, ©Henrik Larsson, ©James Laurie, ©Susan McKenzie, ©Christian Musat, ©ntdanai, ©Perig, ©Alexander Raths, ©Wong Sei Hoo, ©Serhly Shullye, ©Peter Waters, ©weter 777/Shutterstock.com

3-D model art: Steve Roberts/Wildlife art (Tarantula, Black Widow Spider, Sunset Moth, Honeybee);
©Marco Uliana/Shutterstock.com (Spotted Flower Beetle)

Contents

What Is an Insect?	4
Sense-sational	6
Oh, Baby!	8
Presto, Change-o!	10
What's for Dinner?	12
Home Is Where the Larva Is	14
Many Legs Make Light Work	16
Masters of Disguise	18
What Is a Spider?	20
Spiders, Inside Out	22
Body Language	24
Spider Cycle	26
Sensational Silk	28
Hunters and Ambushers	30
Time to Eat!	32
Staying Off the Menu	34
Glossary	36
3-D Puzzle Instructions	38
Diorama Instructions	40

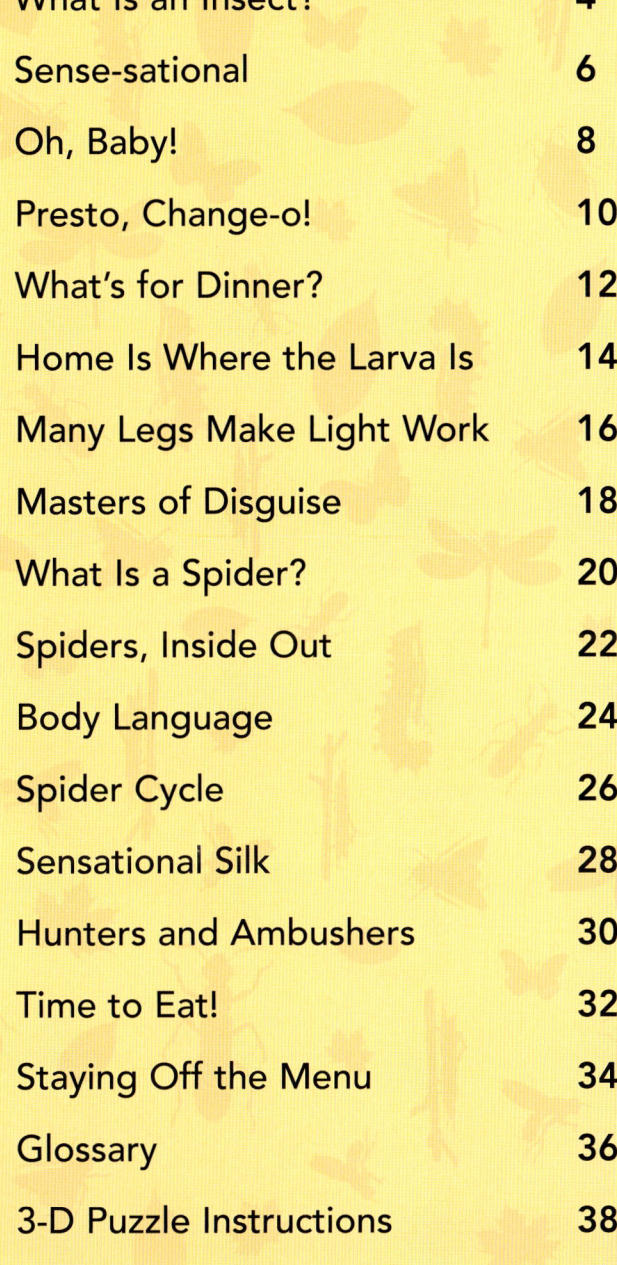

What Is an Insect?

You see them all around you—in the trees, underground, in the water, even in your house. They are insects, and we share the world with 30 million of them! But what are insects?

All insects have several things in common. They all belong to a group of animals called **arthropods**. Instead of bones like you have, they have a tough outer shell called an **exoskeleton**. The exoskeleton is very light and strong and protects the insect's insides.

Every insect's body is divided into three parts: the head, thorax, and abdomen.

Abdomen
The abdomen contains the stomach, heart, air sacs, and other organs.

What's That Word?

As you read, you will see words that are in **bold** type. Look for them in the glossary on pages 36–37 to learn what they mean.

The head has the eyes, antennae, mouthparts, and brain. The head is attached to the thorax. The insect's wings and six legs are attached to the thorax. The abdomen holds all the guts.

Now that you know the basics, let's get to know some of our creeping, crawling neighbours better!

Did You Know?
Cockroaches were among the very first land insects. Scientists have found cockroach fossils that are up to 300 million years old!

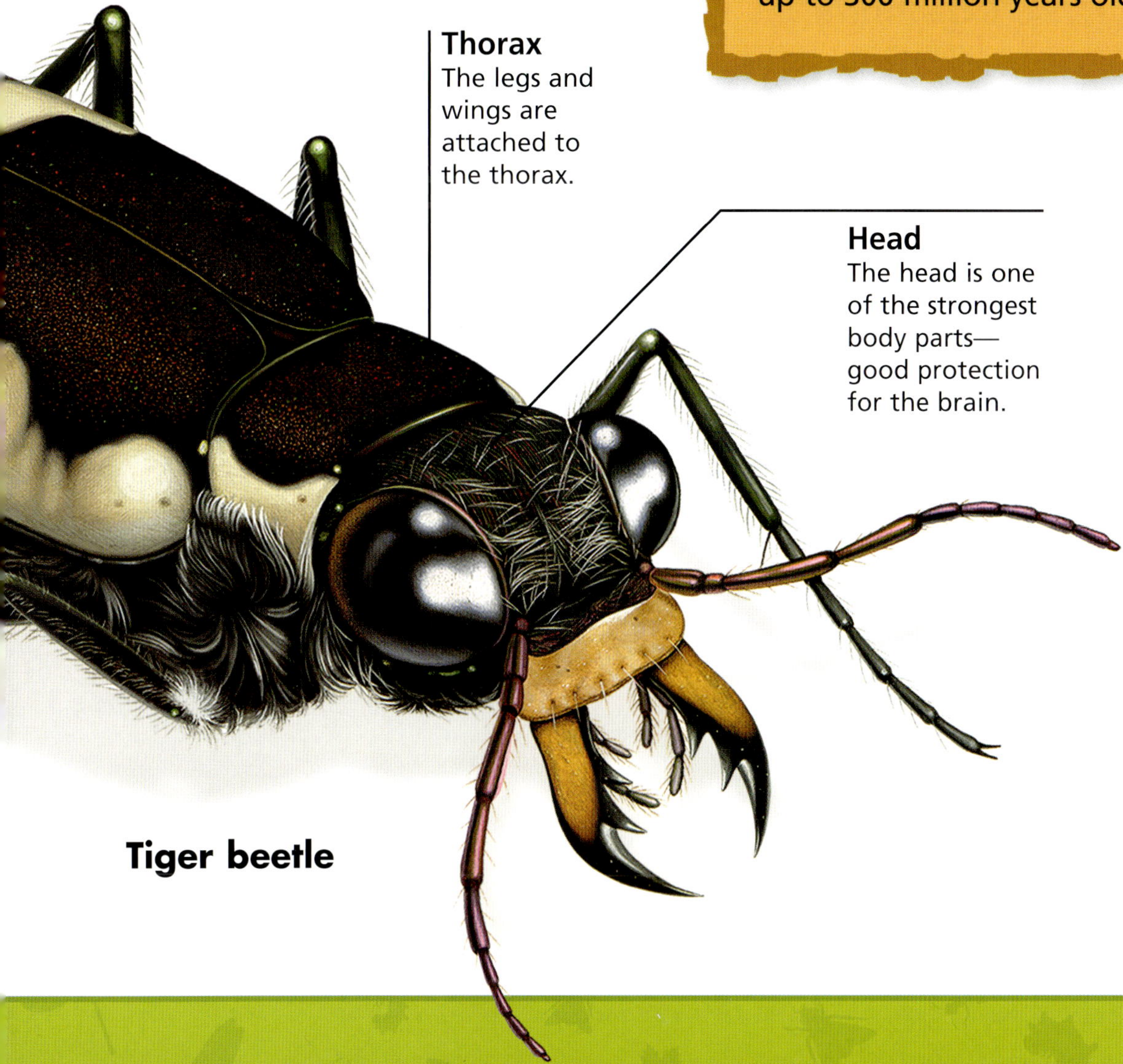

Thorax
The legs and wings are attached to the thorax.

Head
The head is one of the strongest body parts—good protection for the brain.

Tiger beetle

Sense-sational

Insects have the same senses as you do—smell, touch, sight, taste, and hearing. But what parts do they have for using their senses? Do insects have ears? Tongues?

The antennae are two of the most important parts of an insect's body. Antennae are used to smell, touch, and hear. When it comes to seeing, insects have two eyes, like you. But each eye is made up of many little lenses. This lets the insect see all around its body—even the smallest movement.

Insects taste their food before eating by using sense organs near the mouth called **palps**. Some insects, like butterflies and flies, can taste through their feet—letting them know when something they land on is good to eat. Instead of ears, many insects use their antennae and fine body hairs to hear.

The Heat Is On

Female mosquitoes need to drink blood to make eggs. Finding a blood donor is easy for mosquitoes. They are very sensitive to animal scents, body heat, and carbon dioxide—a gas that animals breathe out.

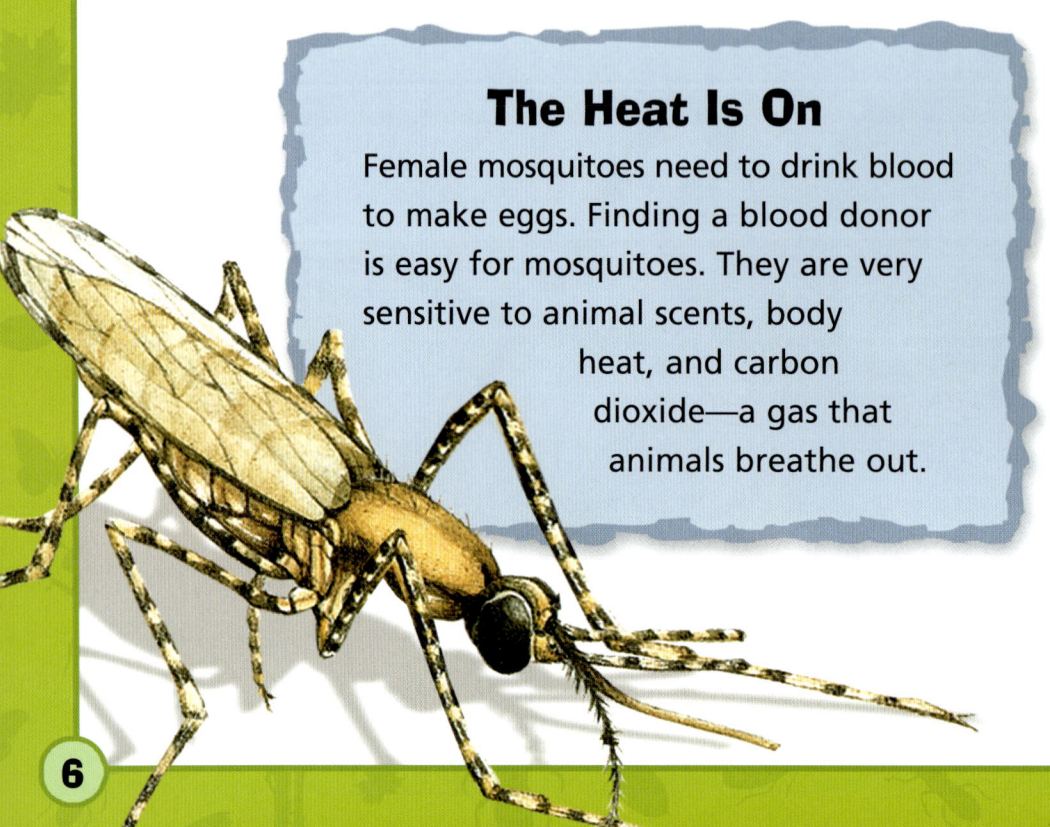

Super Scent Sensors

See those things that look like antlers on this cockchafer beetle's head? Those are very sensitive antennae that can "smell" a female cockchafer beetle from kilometres away. The males use this scent to find mates.

This green darner depends almost entirely on its huge compound eyes to hunt. There are about 28,000 small lenses in each eye.

Oh, Baby!

When it comes to reproducing, insects are pros! Every insect begins life as an egg. Most eggs are laid near plenty of food so that the young have lots to eat when they are born. Insect babies grow quickly, but their exoskeletons can't. They must shed, or **moult**, their old exoskeletons to grow. Each time they moult, they get bigger and change shape. Once they are adults, they stop moulting. This process is called **metamorphosis**.

Some insects look a little like their parents when they are born. They are called nymphs. They go through a simple metamorphosis to grow, changing gradually until they become adults. Some nymphs—like aphids and bedbugs—look just like their parents. Others look very different—and even live in different environments. For example, dragonfly nymphs (called naiads) live underwater. They crawl onto land for their last moult and, after drying off, they fly away!

Did You Know?

Ladybirds lay their eggs on leaves where aphids feed. As soon as a larva hatches, it quickly starts gobbling all the aphids in sight. It will eat about 400 of them before turning into an adult.

Roly-poly Nursery

Dung beetles lay their eggs in a very strange place—on animal pooh! After carefully rolling dung into a ball, the female lays one egg inside. Eventually, the larva will hatch inside its nursery and enjoy its first meal—dung.

Painted grasshoppers use sound to attract females. They rub pegs on their hind legs against ridges on their wings to make a loud rasping noise. The females hear the males' songs and choose a mate.

Presto, Change-o!

Some insect babies look absolutely nothing like their parents. These insects don't change shape gradually. They do it all at once—in a process called complete metamorphosis. When they hatch, they are called larvae. They have soft bodies, no wings, and sometimes have no legs, either! Butterfly and moth larvae are usually called caterpillars. Most fly larvae are called maggots, and most beetle larvae are called grubs.

A larva eats nonstop, and moults several times. Once it is full-sized, it stops eating and moving. This means it's ready to pupate—or finally change into an adult. The larva may become a **pupa** or spin a **cocoon**. During this stage, its body forms all the adult features. When it is finished, it has wings and the ability to reproduce. The new butterfly, beetle, or fly will often eat different foods and live in a different habitat than it did when it was a larva. It's a major change of life!

Did You Know?
Each silkworm cocoon is made of a single thread of silk that can be up to 900 metres long (that's almost a kilometre)! Silk makers boil silkworm cocoons to harvest their silk thread and make it into cloth.

Eggs

Caterpillar

Cocoon

Indian moon moth

This picture shows all the life stages of the Indian moon moth—from egg to new moth. After it leaves the cocoon, the moth must let its new wings stretch and harden before flying for the first time.

Eaten Alive!

A female wasp laid eggs inside this hornworm caterpillar. The larvae hatched and hungrily ate the caterpillar from the inside out. Then they burst through its skin and turned into the white pupae you see here.

What's for Dinner?

So, what do insects eat? That depends on the insect, of course. Many insects feast on plants. Caterpillars and grasshoppers have developed very strong jaws to chew on the leaves they eat. Most termites prefer to eat the woody parts of plants, while some beetle grubs prefer to eat rotting wood and seeds. South American heliconian butterflies like to drink urine!

Insects may also make meals of other insects or small animals like spiders, snails, and tadpoles. Some hunters, like the tiger beetle, may run after their prey. Others, like the praying mantis, sit quietly waiting for lunch to walk close enough to grab. Still others trap their prey. The ant lion larva forms a funnel-shaped trap as it buries itself in sand and waits for an ant. It tosses up sand to make the ant topple down the funnel and into its jaws. Some insects, like mosquitoes, prefer to drink blood.

Super Sippers
Most moths and butterflies have a special mouthpart called a **proboscis**. Shaped like a drinking straw, the proboscis lets these insects sip on the nectar deep inside flowers. Some moths have no mouthparts at all. They live only long enough to breed.

Did You Know?
Praying mantises are fierce and fast **predators.** They usually eat insects, but have been known to catch and eat small lizards or even hummingbirds!

Water scorpions hang upside down beneath the water's surface and wait for prey to swim close. They quickly reach out and grab insect larvae, worms, or even tadpoles with their front legs, then suck out the bodily fluids with a tubelike mouthpart.

Home Is Where the Larva Is

Where is home when you are an insect? Well, it could be under the ground, in a plant stem, or underwater. For some insects, a simple hole or burrow will do. Several larvae, like bagworms and caddis flies, use silk to wrap themselves in leaves, tiny pebbles, or sticks to make portable, protective "apartments."

Many insects go a step further and build complex homes using saliva, mud, wax, or even pooh! Ants mix soil with their own spit to make cement that they use when tunnelling underground. Honeybees have glands in their abdomens that make wax. They use the wax to build combs where they keep honey and young bees. Some wasps live in paper houses. They chew wood into a paste and then use their jaws to form little compartments, or **cells**. A coating of saliva makes the nest waterproof.

Ant Plant

The hollow thorns of an acacia tree make a perfect home for one **species** of ant. The ants help the plant by chasing off anything that might harm it—from beetles to cows. They will even prune nearby plants to make sure the acacia gets enough sun.

Did You Know?

Some Chinese legends say that Ts'ai Lun got the idea to invent paper from watching wasps as they chewed wood and mixed it with their own saliva to make paper nests.

Termite nests are made of many rooms, or chambers. Some hold fungus (the termites' food), some serve as nurseries for the young, and others hold waste. The queen's chamber is in the middle, where she is well protected.

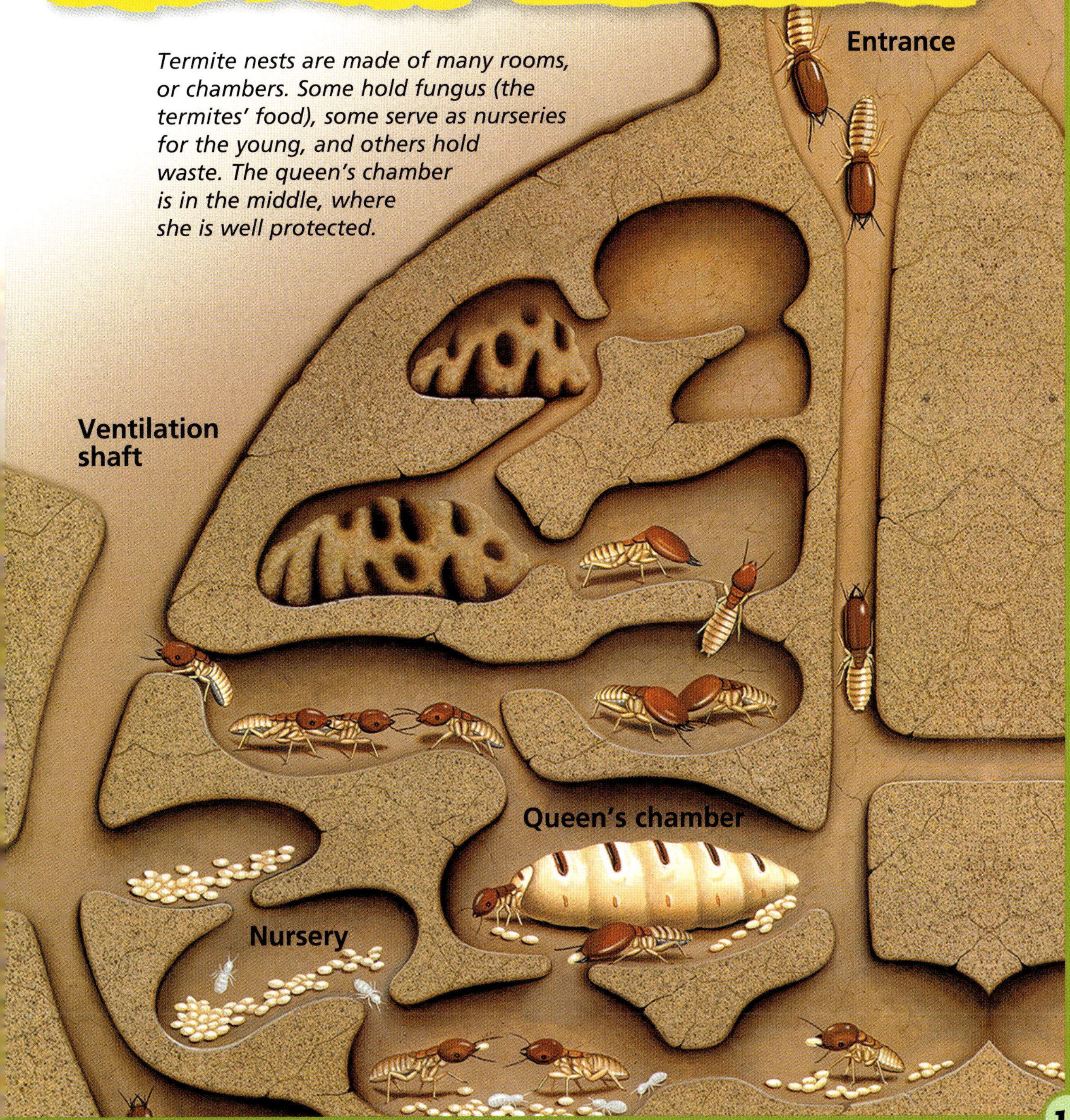

Entrance

Ventilation shaft

Queen's chamber

Nursery

Many Legs Make Light Work

Some insect homes can be pretty amazing, but even more incredible are the insect communities inside. Most wasps and bees—and all ants and termites—live in groups called colonies. Each **colony** is made up of members that each have a certain job to do. By working together, they are able to protect the nest, provide food for everyone, and raise young.

Ant colonies are good examples of insect communities. Every colony has one queen. Her only job is to lay eggs. There are a few males that mate with the queen and leave soon after. The rest of the ants are females. Large ants, called soldiers, guard the nest. Worker ants have many jobs. They build the nest, look for food, take care of the young, or clean up waste from the colony.

Blind Ambition

Most worker termites are blind, yet they are able to build large, complicated nests like this one. These nests can be 3 metres high and are home to millions of termites!

Did You Know?

A honeybee hive must stay at around 34°C so that the larvae can hatch and grow. When the hive gets too hot, the worker bees will fan their wings to cool it off. If it gets too cold, they huddle together in the nursery to heat it up.

Leaf-cutter ants are among the only creatures on earth (besides humans) that farm their own food. Millions of ants work together to maintain "gardens" of leaves that grow the fungus they eat.

Masters of Disguise

There are insects everywhere, and chances are, you aren't seeing *all* of them. This is because many insects use **camouflage** to stay hidden. Insects have developed ways to look like twigs, dead leaves, flowers, or even small piles of pebbles.

Most insects spend a lot of time on and around plants. It's not surprising that many insects look like plant parts. Some treehoppers have bodies that look like thorns, while the colorful orchid mantis has a body that resembles a delicate pink or white flower. Stick insects are just what they sound like—insects that look like sticks. You probably wouldn't notice a stick insect's eggs, either—they are camouflaged to look like seeds.

Some larvae use camouflage to protect their soft bodies. Caddis fly larvae use silk to cover themselves with tiny pebbles or sand to blend in with their lake-bottom environment. Many cocoons look like dead leaves, hiding the pupa inside.

Dead or Alive?

When you think of butterflies, you probably imagine bright colours and pretty patterns. You probably wouldn't notice this resting Indian leaf butterfly. With wings closed, it looks like a dead leaf. But when open, it is painted in shades of bright orange and blue.

Tricky Stick

Can you spot the insect in this picture? Twig insects are experts at hiding—right out in the open. They can be as small as an ant or almost as long as your arm. Some can even change colours to match their surroundings!

When this leaf insect from Malaysia stays completely still or sways in the breeze among the leaves, it would be very difficult to spot—even for a hungry bird.

What Is a Spider?

Eight legs, eight eyes, sharp fangs. This may sound like a description of an alien from outer space, but these creatures are all around you. They are spiders, and there are about 40,000 different species of them!

Spiders are **arachnids**, and they are related to scorpions, ticks, and mites. Instead of having three body segments like insects, they have two: a **cephalothorax** and an abdomen. All eight legs are connected to the cephalothorax, and many of the organs are in the abdomen. Most spiders have eight eyes, but some have six, four, two, or no eyes at all. Tarantulas can be as large as dinner plates, while some tropical spiders are as small as pinheads.

Did You Know?

This daddy longlegs might look like a spider, but it's not! Also called a harvestman, this leggy arachnid has what appears to be only one body segment, whereas spiders have two.

No matter what their size, all spiders are predators. All spiders have fangs—and some can inject a deadly poison into their victims. Spiders eat mainly insects, but some big species can kill and eat scorpions, lizards, small mammals, and even birds.

Marbled orb weaver

Spiders, Inside Out

What's inside a spider's compact body? Lots of the same things that you'd find in yours! Spiders have a brain, a heart, muscles, a stomach, and even a special kind of lung.

A spider's organs do the same things yours do. The brain and nerve cord control all of the body's movements and functions. The heart pumps blood to all the organs. The stomach breaks food down into nutrients for the body to use. Food is first drawn into the sucking stomach, and then it moves into the midgut (similar to your intestines).

Spiders—like insects, mammals, birds, and fish—need oxygen in order to live. Air filters through a pair of organs called **book lungs** in the abdomen. Once inside the body, oxygen seeps into the blood. Some spiders have one pair of book lungs, while others have two.

Fang-tastic!

All spiders have mouthparts called **chelicerae**. There are two types—ones with fangs that move downward (top) and ones with fangs that move together (bottom).

Brown badge huntsman

22

Also in the abdomen are organs called spinnerets. Located near the spider's behind, these organs squirt silk. Other arthropods make silk, but only spiders produce it in every life stage.

Eye Spy

Wolf spiders like this one have eight eyes—two large eyes and six smaller ones. Because this spider actively hunts its food, it has very good eyesight and also has an amazing sense of touch.

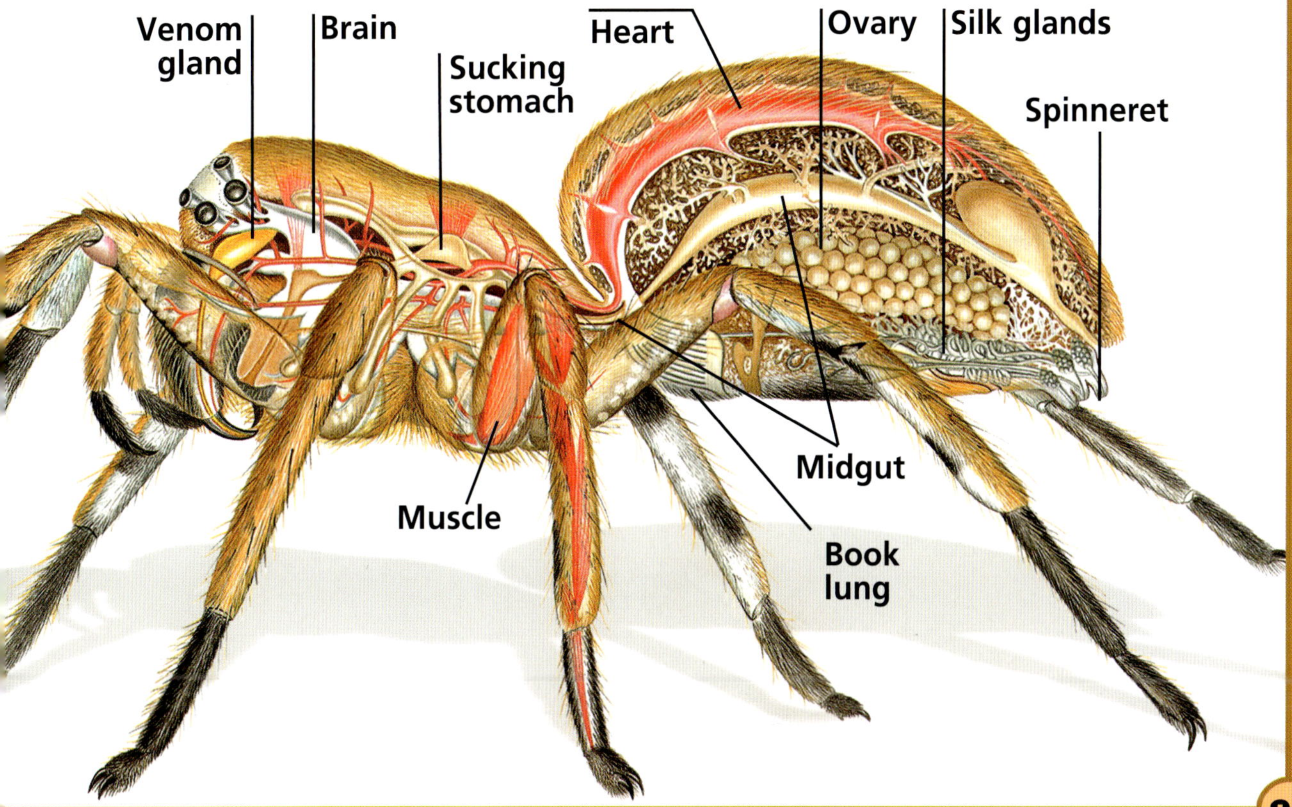

Venom gland | Brain | Sucking stomach | Heart | Ovary | Silk glands | Spinneret | Midgut | Book lung | Muscle

Body Language

Spiders have the same needs as all other living creatures: to find food, to find a mate, and to keep from being eaten. Their senses help them do all these things. A spider sees through a group of eyes along the front of its cephalothorax. In certain spiders, such as jumping spiders, the middle pair of eyes focus on an image, while the rest of the eyes notice even the smallest movement. Many spiders can't see well and depend on body hairs to "see" and sense the world. Some hairs sense movement—on the ground, in the air, or on the water's surface. Other hairs—especially on the **pedipalps** and legs—are used to smell and to taste.

Spiders use their sense organs to communicate with each other, too. Male wolf spiders dance to attract females. Several kinds of spiders coat their silk in **pheromones** to send special scent messages to others of their species. Some use vibrations to talk to possible mates by tapping messages on their webs with their legs or pedipalps.

This male jumping spider is trying to get a female's attention by showing off his colours and patterns in a special dance. If the female is interested, they will mate.

Friend, Not Food!

The male black widow spider (right) is much smaller than the female. He must be careful when walking on her web. She might think he's food! He taps a message on the silk to let her know he'd like to mate.

Spider Cycle

It's a rough world out there for spider babies, but most spider mums do their best to give their young a good start. All spiders lay eggs—there may be only a few eggs or thousands of them—and wrap them in a silk sac. This keeps the eggs protected and safe from **parasites**. Many mothers carry this sac with them until the eggs are ready to hatch; other mothers protect the sac in a web or burrow. Some females die soon after laying their eggs. These spiders simply camouflage their sacs and leave them hidden from enemies.

Once the **spiderlings** have hatched, they huddle together. After a few days, they leave the nest. If they didn't separate, they'd eat each other! They may simply crawl to new homes or "balloon" to new areas. To balloon, a young spider points its abdomen into the air and lets out a strand of silk. The wind catches the silk and carries the spider away. Spiders can travel quite far this way.

Growing Pains

In order to grow, spiders must moult their exoskeletons. Depending on the species, a spider may moult up to 30 times during its life.

After leaving its old exoskeleton, a spider's body is very soft. It must stay hidden until its new exoskeleton hardens.

Did You Know?

A mother wolf spider carries all her newly hatched spiderlings on her back. Special hairs on her abdomen help them get a good grip. There may be as many as 200 spiderlings riding piggyback!

This nursery-web spider carries her egg sac with her everywhere she goes. Just before the eggs hatch, she builds a special nursery by wrapping silk around the stems and leaves of a plant. Then she stands guard to protect her family from enemies.

Sensational Silk

One of the most interesting things about spiders is their ability to make silk. Silk is made in special glands in the spider's abdomen and is almost as strong as steel of the same thickness. It's also very stretchy. Scientists have learned that there are seven different kinds of spider silk. Each is good for a specific purpose—wrapping prey or eggs, lining burrows, making trip wires, and, of course, building webs.

Most spiders that build webs are trying to catch prey. The webs are hard to see and are made from sticky strands. Insects that fly into the web stay put while the hungry spider rushes out to wrap its prey in silk for safekeeping. Funnel-web spiders build tube-shaped webs on the ground. When the spider feels the vibrations of a passing insect on its web, it attacks. Other spiders don't make webs at all because they hunt their prey.

Did You Know?

Silk is liquid until it hits air. The spider pulls the liquid silk out of spigots on the spinnerets. Several strands come out at once, and the spinnerets work like fingers to weave the strands together into a sheet, band, or thread.

This African signature spider is waiting on her web for her next meal. The prey will stick to the web, but the spider won't. She built the web with a frame of nonsticky silk, which she always steps on.

Building an Orb Web

The first fork

Frame completed

Radial threads attached

Frame spiral of dry silk in place

Spiral of sticky silk added

Hunters and Ambushers

All spiders are meat eaters, but the method used to catch food varies from species to species. Most spiders trap prey, but about 18,000 species hunt their food or wait for something to **ambush**.

Most hunting spiders eat beetles, ants, or even other spiders. But some big spiders—like tarantulas and huntsmen—can grab and kill frogs, lizards, small rodents, or birds. Many spiders have a hunting territory. Wolf spiders will chase off any other spiders that try to move in on their hunting grounds. Jumping spiders have amazing eyesight and can see an insect 20 cm away. They attack by leaping onto their prey.

Spiders that ambush rely on not being seen. The trapdoor spider hides in its nest underground. When it senses prey nearby, it flips open its camouflaged "trapdoor" and grabs lunch. Crab spiders can change colours to blend in with the flowers they hunt on—surprising flies and bees.

Did You Know?
People once thought that wolf spiders hunted in packs and worked together to catch prey—as wolves do. That is how these amazing hunters got their name.

Gone Fishing

Fishing spiders will hold onto land or plants with their back legs and dangle their front legs on the water's surface. When they feel vibrations of passing prey, they dive into the water to grab it!

Mexican red-kneed tarantulas have very poor eyesight, and use organs on their legs to pick up vibrations from prey. They attack quickly with fangs that are about one cm long!

Time to Eat!

When it comes to finding something for dinner, spiders have ingenious ways of using silk. Diving-bell spiders build dining rooms out of silk underwater. Once the room is constructed, the spider fills it with air from the surface. The spider leaves to hunt and brings dinner home to be eaten in the air pocket. Some spiders make traplines that hang from simple webs. The lines are stretched onto the ground and have sticky ends. When an insect walks onto a trapline, it snaps back, with the victim dangling in the air.

Once a spider gets its prey, it has an interesting way of eating. A spider can't swallow solid pieces of food. Instead, it **paralyses** its victim with venom and then vomits in strong juices that turn the insides of its prey to liquid. This makes it easy for the spider to suck it up through its small mouth. Almost all spiders must eat this way.

Dangling for Dinner
Bolas spiders like this one eat only one kind of insect—armyworm moths. The spiders attract the moths with a female moth scent. When a male moth flies by, the bolas spider swings a silk thread that has a sticky glob on the end. It sticks onto the moth, and the spider reels it in!

Dinner to Go

After paralysing her grasshopper prey with a fast bite, this spider quickly wraps it in bands of thick silk. Once her catch is wrapped, the spider can store it until she is ready to eat.

This ogre-faced spider hangs from a branch and waits for an insect to crawl by. When it spots one with its large eyes, the spider throws a small elastic web—like a fishing net—over its prey to trap it.

Staying Off the Menu

What's to worry about when you are a spider? Getting eaten! Birds are probably the biggest threat, but lizards, toads, small mammals, and even other spiders also enjoy spiders for lunch.

How do spiders stay alive? That depends on the spider. Some simply stay out of sight when they aren't hunting. Others will suddenly drop from their webs if approached, hoping their attacker won't spot them dangling below. Many spiders use camouflage to blend in with their surroundings or **mimic** other, more dangerous animals, like wasps. The South African white lady spider curls its legs under its body and quickly rolls down sand and dunes to escape trouble.

Some spiders—like spiny orb weavers—have sharp spikes on their bodies, so birds stay away from them. Tarantulas can flick barbed hairs at attackers, sending even larger enemies running.

Did You Know?

Female green lynx spiders are very protective of their egg sacs. If a predator gets too close, she will spit powerful venom from her fangs. She can spit as far as 20 cm!

Don't Touch!

No one likes to eat pooh. That's why this spider is safe out in the open—even during the day. Her body is coloured and shaped like a pile of bird droppings, keeping her hidden from even the hungriest predator.

When a predator, like this giant centipede, barges into a trapdoor spider's burrow, the spider runs into its secret room and pulls the door shut. Unable to find the spider, the centipede eventually leaves.

Glossary

ambush: An ambush is a surprise attack. When a spider ambushes prey, it hides until its victim gets close, then quickly grabs it.

arthropod: An animal with jointed legs and an exoskeleton. This group of animals includes insects, spiders, crabs, scorpions, centipedes, millipedes, ticks, and mites.

arachnid: A creature that has eight jointed legs and two body segments, but has no antennae or wings. Spiders, mites, ticks, and scorpions belong to this group.

book lung: A book lung is used for breathing. It is made of many flat sheets, like the pages of a book. This helps the spider get lots of oxygen.

camouflage: Colours, body shapes, or patterns that make an animal blend in with its surroundings.

cell: A small compartment. Honeybees and some wasps make nests that are made up of many individual cells. Most cells are used to store food or a single egg. The word "cell" comes from the Latin *cella*, which means "storeroom" or "chamber."

cephalothorax: Instead of a separate head and thorax, spiders have a cepaholothorax that includes both.

chelicerae: A spider's mouthparts, used for grabbing and sometimes crushing prey. Each chelicera has a sharp fang that can inject venom into prey.

cocoon: A covering of silk, mud, wood, or leaves. It protects the developing pupa inside. The word "cocoon" comes from *coco*, a French word for "shell."

colony: A group of animals of the same species that live and work together.

exoskeleton: This word comes from the Greek words *exo*, which means "outside," and *skeletos*, which means "dried up" or "hard." An insect's exoskeleton is made of many pieces that are joined with a softer material that helps it bend.

metamorphosis: The sometimes drastic change of shape that all insects go through to grow. Two Greek words—*meta*, meaning "change," and *morphe,* meaning "form" or "shape"—make up this word.

mimic: A creature that copies or acts like another animal is a mimic. Insect and spider mimics fool attackers into thinking they are dangerous or poisonous animals when they are not. This keeps them from being eaten.

moult: The process spiders, insects, and other arthropods use to grow. When a creature moults, it sheds the outer layer (or exoskeleton) of its body.

palp: A sense organ near the mouth that an insect uses to taste its food. This word comes from the Latin *palpare*, which means "to feel."

paralyse: When something is paralysed, it can't move. Most spiders have a paralysing venom that keeps their prey from struggling while being eaten.

parasite: A plant or animal that lives or feeds off another plant or animal (called a host). Usually the parasite doesn't kill its host, but makes it very sick.

pedipalp: A spider has two pedipalps near its mouth. They are used to touch, taste, and smell.

pheromone: A pheromone is a scent used by some animals to communicate with others of its species. Pheromones attract mates or warn others of danger.

predator: An animal or insect that hunts other animals to eat.

proboscis: A mouthpart shaped like a straw that is found on butterflies, honeybees, mosquitoes, and some other insects. It is used to suck up liquid food (like nectar or blood).

pupa: A stage that an insect goes through to finish complete metamorphosis. While a pupa, the insect's body parts break down and adult features form. *Pupa* is the Latin word for "doll."

species: A group of living things (plants or animals) that have enough in common to be able to reproduce.

spiderling: Baby spiders right after they hatch from eggs.

3-D Model Instructions

Complete one model at a time. Press out the pieces and arrange them as shown. Using the numbers on the pictures here, match the slots and assemble your 3-D insects and spiders.

Mexican Red-kneed Tarantula

Some tarantulas can live as long as 30 years.

Black Widow Spider

Adult female black widows are the most venomous spiders in the U.S.

38

Sunset Moth
Most moths fly at night, but the sunset moth is active during the day.

Honeybee
Each bee makes 1/12 teaspoon of honey in its lifetime.

Spotted Flower Beetle
These beetles feed on the nectar and pollen from flowers.

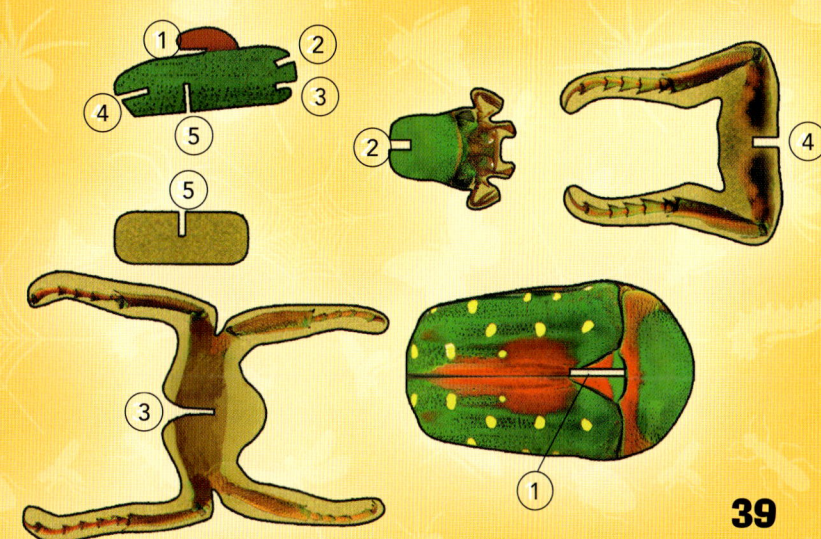

39

Diorama Instructions

Create your own insect and spider environment by building a beautiful diorama. It's easy!

1. The inside of the box lid and base will be the walls of your diorama. The unfolding board will be the floor. Decorate these with reusable stickers as desired.

2. Press out the floor figures, and fold as shown. Fold, then slide the rectangular tabs through the floor slots, folding them underneath so the figures stand upright. The tabs and slots are all the same size, so you can change the position of the figures.

3. Stand the box lid and base upright and at an angle as shown. Lay the angled back edges of the floor piece on top of the box sides. You're done!

box base

box lid

stickers

unfolding board

floor figures

40